BIOGRAPHY

OF

AYMAN AL-ZAWAHIRI

Zuhair Kassem seif

All right reserved. No part of this book publication should

be reproduced, distributed, or transmitted in any form or

by any means without any form of

Written permission.

Copyright ©2022 **Zuhair Kassem seif**.

TABLE OF CONTENT

Chapter 1

Who is Ayman Al-Zawahiri

Al-Zawahiri, 71, was the head of al-Qaeda; Americans were familiar with him as Osama bin Laden's bespectacled and bushy-bearded deputy. However, the truth is that the most notorious terrorist movement in the world was led by Ayman al-Zawahiri, whose hands were covered in blood.

According to officials with knowledge of the situation who spoke on the condition of anonymity to discuss sensitive intelligence, Zawahiri, 71, was killed in a CIA drone strike in Kabul over the weekend. President Biden announced the death in a speech to the country, calling the assault a "precise strike" that didn't harm civilians.

Zawahiri founded his terrorist organization and was the father of a style of terrorism that emphasized spectacular attacks and the indiscriminate killing of innocent. He brought these strategies and a wider plan for targeting the West with him when he formally united his organization with al-Qaeda in the 1990s.

To take on al-Qaeda's enemy," the pro-Western Arab regimes that stood in the way of the organization's aspiration to unify all Muslims under a global caliphate,

Zawahiri posited that it was crucial to first defeat the "far enemy," or the United States.

In a 1998 manifesto, Zawahiri stated that "killing Americans and their supporters, civilian and military, is an individual duty for any Muslim who can do it in every place in which is feasible to put it into action. Three years later, on September 11, 2001, his involvement in the preparation for the Pentagon and World Trade Center attacks would lead to his words being put into action.

Zawahiri became the intellectual driving force behind much of al-Qaeda's biggest aspirations, including its ostensibly fruitless attempts to acquire nuclear and biological weapons, although missing Bin Laden's charm. Longtime al-Qaeda analysts claim that Zawahiri was largely responsible for the terrorist organization's comeback in the lawless tribal region of Pakistan after the group was forcibly driven from its base in Afghanistan in early 2002.

Zawahiri presided over al-Qaeda in his later years during a period of decline, when the majority of the organization's original members were either dead or in hiding and the leadership of the group was under threat from abrasive upstarts like the Islamic State.

Despite being the leader of the terrorist organization, he was powerless to stop the Islamist movement from splintering in Syria and other hotspots after 2011. He was rumoured to be in poor health, and he gained notoriety for his protracted disappearances from the public eye, which were sporadically broken by the publication of essays, books, and sermon videos that displayed his recognizable dry, pedantic style—unfit for the social media era.

Bruce Riedel, a veteran CIA counterterrorism analyst and advisor to four U.S. presidents, stated in a September interview that Zawahiri is the ideology of al-Qaeda and is more of a thinker than an actor. He writes in a ponderous and occasionally unbearably monotonous manner.

The ability of Zawahiri to direct events or exercise leadership within the widely dispersed jihadist movement appeared to be waning as the second decade following 9/11 drew to a close, Riedel added. He claimed that neither he nor anybody else on the horizon was the charismatic leader that al-Qaeda required.

Chapter 2

His Path to terrorism and Escape to Pakistan

Zawahiri's route to becoming one of the most well-known terrorists in the world had an unexpected beginning in an upper-middle-class, religiously mixed Cairo suburb that was home to many of Egypt's most affluent families.

Zawahiri's maternal grandfather served as president of Cairo University, and his father, Mohammed Rabie al-Zawahiri, was a professor of pharmacology. Zawahiri was born on June 19, 1951, in Maadi, which at the time of his birth had a sizable Jewish population as well as more churches than mosques.

He was an earnest, academically talented young man who was influenced early in life by Sayyid Qutb, an Egyptian author and intellectual who is credited with being one of the founders of 20th-century Islamist extremism, as well as by one of his uncles, Mahfouz Azzam, an ardent critic of Egypt's secularist government. According to Lawrence Wright's account in his Pulitzer Prize-winning book "The Looming Tower," Zawahiri, who was 15 at the time, was motivated to gather a group of young friends into an underground cell to overthrow the Egyptian government and establish an Islamic theocracy after Qutb was executed by the Egyptian government in 1966. Jamaat al-Jihad, also known as the Jihad group, was eventually formed by Zawahiri's small number of supporters.

Zawahiri was pursuing a career in the medical field, getting a degree in medicine from Cairo University, and briefly working as an army physician even as his political views grew more rigid. He finally established practice in a duplex owned by his parents and on occasion provided medical care at a clinic in Cairo supported by the Muslim Brotherhood, a Sunni Islamist political opposition party. He wed Azza Nowair, a politically influential Egyptian family's affluent daughter, and the two went on to have a son and five daughters.

Zawahiri received the first of several invitations to travel to refugee camps along the Afghanistan-Pakistan border when he was employed at the Muslim Brotherhood clinic. He treated the mujahideen battling the Soviets in Afghanistan there, and there he met the charismatic young Saudi who would become Osama bin Laden. But Zawahiri was busy running his revolutionary movement at the moment. The Egyptian President Anwar Sadat was assassinated on October 6, 1981, as a result of a series of plans that His Jihad Group launched in the early 1980s to kill Egyptian leaders.

Hundreds of Zawahiri's supporters were imprisoned as a result of the extensive government crackdown that came after. After serving a three-year sentence, Zawahiri was freed, although he would later write in a memoir that he had been tortured while imprisoned and that this had strengthened his resolve to overthrow the Egyptian government. After leaving prison, Zawahiri lived a nomadic life for several years, frequently visiting South Asia and growing closer to both the mujahideen and bin Laden, who relied on the Egyptian as his doctor. The Saudis needed repeated injections of glucose due to low blood pressure and other chronic conditions. Zawahiri's steadfastness in providing aid in the face of the Soviet bombing of Afghanistan solidified the doctor's standing among the mujahideen and their friendship for life.

During at least one trip to the US in the 1990s, Zawahiri visited California mosques for a short time to gather money for Muslim charities.

assisting Afghan refugees. He persisted in encouraging his supporters in Egypt to carry out greater and more spectacular domestic attacks, reasoning that such brutally cruel measures would grab media attention and drown out more moderate voices who favoured discussion and compromise. 1997 saw him residing in Afghanistan.

During a 45-minute rampage at Egypt's famed Luxor ruins, Zawahiri assisted in organizing a vicious attack on international tourists.

62 individuals, including Japanese visitors, a 5-year-old British girl, and four Egyptian tour guides, lost their lives.

The massacre repulsed common Egyptians, and Zawahiri and his Jihad Group lost support as a result. Soon after, Zawahiri warned his supporters that it was no longer able to conduct operations in Egypt and that the conflict had moved to Israel and its main partner, the United States. The Jihad Group and al-Qaeda, sometimes known as "The Base," bin Laden's more powerful and well-funded organization, officially united.

At the time of the 1998 bombings of the American embassies in the capitals of Kenya and Tanzania, which resulted in the deaths of hundreds of people, Zawahiri served as bin Laden's top advisor. He assisted in the planning of the Sept. 11 attacks in New York and Washington three years later while operating out of al-base Qaeda in Afghanistan, which would go down in history as one of the most daring terrorist operations.

Zawahiri was tasked with organizing subsequent waves of terrorist operations meant to further erode America's economy and resolve as the hijackers from September 11 were sent to start training in American cities. He started a large-scale campaign to develop biological weapons, setting up a lab in Afghanistan and sending followers to look for sympathetic researchers and deadly strains of the anthrax bacteria.

Zawahiri's attempts might have been successful if he hadn't run out of time, according to U.S. intelligence officials. After the World Trade Center buildings in New York City fell, Zawahiri was compelled to close his bioweapons facility after an American-backed military operation ousted al-Taliban Qaeda's allies from power in Afghanistan.

Al-Qaeda officials' residences and offices, including Zawahiri's compound, were struck by American bomber aircraft. After the roof caved in, his wife was left stranded in the debris, but she reportedly refused to be rescued because she was afraid men would see her without her veil. Her hypothermic death was discovered later.

Escape To Pakistan.

Together, Zawahiri and bin Laden fled to the tribal region of Pakistan, where they both went into hiding to avoid detection despite the $25 million price tag placed on their heads. Even though neither man was seen in the ensuing ten years, the CIA reportedly carried out at least two missile attacks within Pakistan in 2006 and 2008 that were believed to have been directed at the Egyptian's most recent residences.

Zawahiri kept popping up in videos that were published on al-Qaeda-friendly websites despite the intensified manhunt. Officials in the United States think he continued to lead multiple terrorist actions, like the Red Mosque siege in Islamabad, Pakistan, in 2007, which left over 100 people dead.

Even while he periodically battled with younger extremists over strategy—arguing that the massacre of Muslims in Iraq had damaged support for al-Qaeda—he never publicly changed his opinion of the West or his support for violent jihad.

He declared in a video from February 2009 that "the entire planet is our field against the targets of the Zionist Crusade." "And it's not the enemy's business to dictate to us where we fight, when we fight, or how we fight," the verse continues.

Zawahiri assumed the top spot after bin Laden's death in May 2011, a position for which, in retrospect, he might not have been the best fit. The Egyptian's dry, academic demeanour failed to compel jihadists in the same way that bin Laden or younger figures like the Jordanian Abu Musab al-Zarqawi, who started the Iraqi insurgency that would eventually become the Islamic State, could do.

After the Arab Spring demonstrations began, Zawahiri tried to seize control of the disparate collection of locally-led Islamist organizations vying for supremacy in Syria, Iraq, and Libya. He would ultimately fail in his endeavour.

The most important al-Qaeda offshoot in Syria, formerly known as the al-Nusra Front, ultimately decided to separate itself from the parent group and refuse to publicly recognize the al-Qaeda moniker. Zawahiri issued a public rebuke after the Islamic State, the other significant component, completely severed ties with him.

Following that, Zawahiri was rarely, if ever, looked to for advice or a resolution to their disagreements as partisans within both organizations would quarrel over strategy, tactics, and even fundamental beliefs.

By 2020, Zawahiri had grown more aloof, satisfied to compose books and essays and occasionally make video appearances. In September 2021, an al-Qaeda supporter's website published a fresh video in which the senile Zawahiri spoke for an hour and made scathing allusions to current news stories as if to refute rumours of his demise.

However, Zawahiri failed to bring up the 20th anniversary of the 9/11 attacks or the Taliban taking over Afghanistan in August, which occurred just one month before the video was released. However, he did make use of the opportunity to revive his vehement rhetoric, urging a continuation of al-Qaeda's assaults against all foes.

We must hit them hard everywhere, he declared in the video, "just as they have gathered from all over the world to fight us."

Chapter 3

Formation Of Al Qaeda

Members of al-Qaeda were attracted from all across the Islamic world to serve as a logistical support network for Muslims engaged in combat with the Soviet Union during the Afghan War. When the Soviets left Afghanistan in 1989, the group disintegrated but kept up its opposition to what its leaders saw as corrupt Islamic regimes and foreign (i.e., American) influence in Islamic countries. Initially based in Sudan in the early 1990s, the organization eventually relocated its headquarters, with the support of the Taliban militia, to Afghanistan (around 1996) Al-Qaeda joined forces with several other violent Islamist groups, such as the Islamic Movement in Egypt and the Islamic group, and multiple times its leaders have vowed a holy war against the United States. Tens of thousands were trained in paramilitary techniques at camps set up by the organization for Muslim militants from around the world, and its agents participated in various terrorist operations, including the burning down of the American embassies in Nairobi, Kenya, and Dar es Salaam, Tanzania (both in 1998), as well as the suicide bombing of the US warship Cole in Aden, Yemen (2000; see USS Cole attack). Nineteen al-Qaeda-affiliated terrorists organized the September 11 attacks against the United States in 2001.

In response, the US administration attacked Taliban and al-Qaeda forces in Afghanistan within a few weeks. Numerous important militants were killed or captured, including the militant who is believed to have planned and organized the September 11 attacks. The remainder of the militant group and their leaders were forced into hiding.

Al- Qaeda's use of Afghanistan as a haven and training ground was put in jeopardy in the wake of the 2001 invasion of the country. Additionally, the links between al-leadership Qaeda and its militants' operations, finances, and lines of communication were jeopardized. However, these facts led to a structural change and a rise in "franchising" rather than dramatically weakening al-Qaeda.

Attacks were increasingly planned by both the regional, largely independent cells that it supported, as well as the centralized leadership that, during the U.S. invasion of Afghanistan, was located in the Afghan-Pakistani border regions. Such local, independent grassroots groups coalesced around a shared cause.

Nonetheless, they support Al-Qaeda and have an agenda therefore, the term and its larger ideology referred to a subtler and much more challenging style of militancy.

With this organizational change, al-Qaeda was connected to more attacks in the six years after September 11 than in the six years before, including attacks in Jordan, Kenya, Saudi Arabia, Indonesia, Turkey, the United Kingdom, Israel, Algeria, and other countries. These attacks occurred in addition to attacks in Jordan, Kenya, Saudi Arabia, Saudi Arabia, Indonesia, Turkey, and other countries. Attacks were increasingly planned not only from above by the centralized leadership (after the U.S. invasion of Afghanistan, located in the Afghan-Pakistani border regions), but also by the localized, mostly independent cells it fostered. Locally, these separate grassroots groups formed around a shared cause.

agenda but supporting Al-Qaeda

name and its larger ideology so meant a more subtle and challenging kind of militancy.

With this organizational change, al-Qaeda was connected to more attacks in the six years that followed September 11 than in the six years before, including attacks in Jordan, Kenya, Saudi Arabia, Indonesia, Turkey, the United Kingdom, Israel, Algeria, and other countries. These attacks were also connected to al-Qaeda, either directly or indirectly. A small team arrived in Abbottabad via helicopter to conduct the mission. Obama praised the operation as a big victory in the war against al-Qaeda once it was established that bin Laden had indeed been killed.

Al-Qaeda announced in a statement on June 16, 2011, that Ayman al-Zawahiri, bin Laden's longtime deputy, had been named to take over as the group's head.

Chapter 4

The Killing Of Al Qaeda leader by US Biden Led
Administration.

During a speech, Biden made at the White House.

"I gave the order to kill him with a precise hit.

once and for all from the battlefield, "said Biden.

11 years after Osama bin Laden was killed by the US,
Zawahiri, who just turned 71, continued to be a prominent
international symbol of the organization. He once took an
action.

serving as bin Laden's doctor.

According to Biden, Zawahiri was seeking refuge in the
heart of Kabul to rejoin his family when he was murdered
in what a senior administration official called "a precision
tailored airstrike" involving two Hellfire missiles.

According to the office on Monday, Biden authorized the
drone strike, which was carried out at 9:48 p.m. ET on
Saturday, after several meetings with his cabinet and key

advisers. No American personnel were present at the scene when the attack occurred in Kabul.

seasoned Haqqani In "clear violation of the Doha agreement," the official stated, that Taliban figures were aware of Zawahiri's presence in the region. They even took action to hide it after Saturday's successful strike, restricting access to the safe house and hastily relocating members of his family, including his daughter and her children, who were purposefully not targeted during the strike and were unharmed. The US did not forewarn officials about the Taliban.

of Saturday's strike. Zabiullah Mujahid, a spokesman for the Taliban, stated in a series of tweets, "An air attack was carried out on a private house in Sherpur neighbourhood of Kabul city on July 31, 2022.

He said that initially "the nature of the incident was not evident," but that after the Islamic Emirate's security and intelligence services looked into it, "initial results showed that the hit was carried out by a drone from the US.

Before the news outlets reported Zawahiri's passing, Mujahid posted the tweets. According to Mujahid, Afghanistan's Islamic Emirate "calls this act a flagrant breach of and strongly condemns it under any excuse.

internationally accepted standards and the Doha Agreement."

Biden spoke outside on Monday from the Blue Room while being quarantined with a rebound case of Covid19, keeping him informed of the attack against Zawahiri.

Zawahiri, according to Biden, "was heavily involved in the planning of 9/11, one of the guys most accountable for the assaults that killed 2,977 people on American soil. He was responsible for attacks for many years.

American citizens

Now that justice has been served, this terrorist commander has been eliminated. No longer in use by people everywhere

need to be terrified of the ruthless and determined murderer," he added. The US continues to show that it is willing and able to protect its citizens from those who would harm them. The United States will find you and eliminate you if you pose a threat to our citizens, no matter how long it takes or where you hide. We are making this point abundantly clear once more tonight.

The President credited the country's intelligence community's "amazing persistence and competence" for the precision strike targeting.

Earlier this year, Zawahiri was discovered by our intelligence community; he had relocated to Kabul to live with his immediate family, Biden added. One year ago, Biden gave the order for US troops to leave Afghanistan, which allowed the Taliban to quickly seize power there. Now, the attack has taken place. During the withdrawal of US forces from Afghanistan, Biden said, "I decided that after 20 years of war, the United States no longer needed thousands of boots on the ground in Afghanistan to protect America from terrorists who seek to do us harm and | made a promise to the American people that we continue to conduct effective counterterrorism operations in Afghanistan." and beyond. We've already taken that action.

Zawahiri "will never again allow Afghanistan to become a terrorist haven, because he is gone and we're going to make sure that nothing happens," Biden promised.

something else takes place. Finally, the President thanked the US intelligence and counterterrorism communities and expressed his thanks, adding that he hoped Zawahiri's passing would provide some measure of closure for the 9/11 friends and families victims.

"I want those who continue to want to harm the United States to know that we will always be watchful, we will take action, and we will always do what is right.

vital to safeguard Americans' safety and security both at home and abroad, "he concluded.

According to a senior counterterrorism specialist, Zawahiri could not have travelled to Kabul without the consent and invitation of at least a few Taliban, whether from the Afghan or Pakistani branches.

Haqqani network or another section of the organization.

The analyst argued that this incident was embarrassing for the Taliban because they had claimed there were no foreign fighters in Afghanistan.

Afghanistan has fighters but not Al Qaeda.

He claimed that recent remarks from Zawahiri had suggested the al Qaeda commander was feeling more at ease. The analyst noted that the statements had referenced more recent occurrences, noting that this might have reflected complacency that may have contributed to the successful strike. The question of who will succeed Zawahiri now emerges.

Saif al Adel, the alleged leader of al Qaeda at the moment, has visited Iran, according to reports from the UN.

According to the analyst, this presents an urgent problem for the Iranians, who must now decide between ejecting the brand-new al Qaeda chief or protecting him.

A former Afghan government official who is well-versed in counterterrorism claimed to have Al Adel was rumoured to have already departed for Afghanistan.

Bin Laden's close friend

According to the New York Times, Zawahiri is descended from a prominent Egyptian family. Rabia'a al-Zawahiri, his grandfather, was an imam at Cairo's al-Azhar University.

Abdel Rahman, his great-uncle, the Arab League's first secretary was Azzam.

Later, when the hijackers switched sides and carried out the bloodiest terror attack on American soil, he assisted in planning it.

"God Almighty has granted them this triumph we are relishing now to those 19 brothers who went forth and devoted their souls to Allah Almighty," al-Zawahiri said in a statement.

released in April 2002, a videotaped message.

The terrorist sent the first of numerous taunting messages with this one.

over the years, encouraging militants to continue the fight against America. -who took over as al Qaeda's leader after US forces killed bin Laden in 2011-would send-out.reprimanding US officials, too.

After September 11, 2001, attacks, Zawahiri was never still as the US-led invasion of Afghanistan got underway. He narrowly evaded a US assault at one point in Afghanistan's rough, hilly Tora Bora region; the raid left his wife and deceased children.

While incarcerated for his role in the 1981 Iranian revolution, he made his first appearance in public as a Muslim militant.

President Anwar Sadat of Egypt was assassinated.

"We want to address the entire planet. So who are we?

So who are we? "He said during a prison interview.

Young doctor al-Zawahiri was already a devoted terrorist at that point. He had been plotting for years to topple the Egyptian government and install a fundamentalist Islamic government in its place. After Sadat was killed, he enthusiastically supported the leader's settlement with Israel.

For over 3years he was imprisoned.

Assassination and that he had been tortured while being held captive. After being freed, he travelled to Pakistan to provide medical care for mujahadeen combatants who fought against the Soviet occupation of Afghanistan.

He encountered bin Laden and discovered a common Origin.

"When Egyptian Islamic Jihad merged with al Qaeda in May 1998, Osama bin Laden declared, "We are cooperating with brother bin Laden. "For over ten years now, both of us have known each other. We fought against unbelievers here in Afghanistan with him.

Bin Laden and Zawahiri were happy when they avoided a retaliatory cruise missile attack by the US in Afghanistan.

Then there was the attack on the USS Cole in Yemen in October 2000, when suicide attackers on a dinghy exploded their boat, killing 17 American sailors and injuring dozens more 38 other people were wounded.

On September 11, 2001, when the Pentagon and World Trade Center twin towers were attacked, Zawahiri's terrorist plot came to a head and over 3,000 people perished. In a Pennsylvania field, a fourth hijacked plane that was en route to Washington crashed following resistance from the passengers.

Al-Zawahiri has now gained further notoriety by appearing on several videos and audiotapes and pleading with Muslims to join the jihad against the US and its allies. Attacks by terrorists occurred soon after some of his tapes.

For example, in May 2003, days after a tape allegedly including Zawahiri's voice was made public, two almost simultaneous suicide bombs in Riyadh, Saudi Arabia, resulted in the deaths of 23 individuals, including nine Americans.

The US State Department had provided an incentive of up to. 25millionUS dollars for information that may lead to his capture, up to. He may have been found in the area between Afghanistan and Pakistan, according to a June 2021 United Nations report, to be used in propaganda because they were too weak.

Gratitude is expressed by the 9/11 relatives group, but they want Biden to hold Saudi Arabia responsible.

The head of 9/11 Relatives United, a group of victims' families and survivors of the September 11, 2001, terrorist attacks, Terry Strada, expressed his gratitude for the strike but urged the President to hold the Saudi Arabian government accountable for Supposed government involvement in the attacks.

The team has slammed the Saudi-sponsored LIV Golf circuit, which kicked off its third event at Trump National Golf Club Bedminster at the end of July.

50 miles away from Ground Zero in Manhattan.

"I'm incredibly appreciative of the effort and sacrifices made by our courageous military, intelligence agencies, and intelligence professionals in eliminating such evil from our world. But to obtain complete restitution for the killing of thousands on Sept.

"Drones are not used to target the bankers; instead, they are welcomed at golf clubs and given fist bumps. If we're going to take accountability seriously, we need to hold EVERYONE accountable, "Strada continued, seemingly referring to the President's divisive gesture toward Saudi Crown Prince Mohammed bin Salman.

www.ingramcontent.com/pod-product-compliance
Lightning Source LLC
Chambersburg PA
CBHW070734160726
48003CB00006BA/2499